3-26-19
AR 5.1

Danvers Township Library
117 E. Exchange Street
Danvers, IL 61732-0376
PH/FAX 309-963-4269
www.danverstownshiplibrary.com

Eerie Parks and Playgrounds

by Joyce Markovics

Consultant: Debbie Felton
Professor of Classics
University of Massachusetts
Amherst, Massachusetts

BEARPORT
PUBLISHING

New York, New York

Credits

Cover, © enolabrain/Fotolia, © Nadezhda Bolotina/Fotolia, © k_kron/Fotolia, © iordani/Fotolia, © Cheryl Casey/Fotolia, © Sergey Khamidulin/Fotolia, and © Alexander Mirokhin/Fotolia; 4–5, © lucag_g/Fotolia, © pavlovski/Fotolia, © pavlovski/Fotolia, © magmac83/Fotolia © bruno135_406/Fotolia, and © blantiag/Fotolia; 6, © Eduardo Carneglia; 7, © AlexLinch/iStock; 8, © Floyd Stewart; 9, © Underwood Archives/AGE Fotostock; 10, © Jackson County Historical Society; 11T, © IgorGolovniov/Shutterstock; 11B, © NOAA.gov; 12, © Omaha World-Herald; 13, © Ken Eakins; 14, © Smallbones/CC0; 15, © fotoslaz/Shutterstock; 16, © Stephen Krystopowicz; 17, © neoblues/iStock; 18, © CaptainK/CC BY 4.0; 19, © Tom Tom/Shutterstock; 20, © Len Holsborg/Alamy; 21, © Everett Collection Historical/Alamy; 22, © Agnus McComiskey/Alamy; 23, © Lario Tus/Shutterstock; 24, © imgur.com; 25, © Vizerskaya/iStock; 26, © Anthony Ricci/Shutterstock; 27, © aleks1949/iStock; 31, © bfnmtspc/Shutterstock; 32, © Wisa Thanarimit/Shutterstock.

Publisher: Kenn Goin
Senior Editor: Joyce Tavolacci
Creative Director: Spencer Brinker
Design: Dawn Beard Creative
Cover: Kim Jones
Photo Researcher: Thomas Persano

Library of Congress Cataloging-in-Publication Data in process at time of publication (2019)
Library of Congress Control Number: 2018047320
ISBN-13: 978-1-64280-172-9

Copyright © 2019 Bearport Publishing Company, Inc. All rights reserved. No part of this publication may be reproduced in whole or in part, stored in any retrieval system, or transmitted in any form or by any means, electronic, mechanical, photocopying, recording, or otherwise, without written permission from the publisher.

For more information, write to Bearport Publishing Company, Inc., 45 West 21st Street, Suite 3B, New York, New York 10010. Printed in the United States of America.

10 9 8 7 6 5 4 3 2 1

Contents

Eerie Parks and Playgrounds 4
A Spooky Swing 6
Haunted Hawaii 8
A Deadly Storm 10
Watch Your Step! 12
Grave Matters 14
Creepy in Connecticut 16
Sick to Death 18
Garden of Good and Evil 20
Troubled Waters 22
Dead Children's Playground 24
The Skunk Ape 26

Eerie Parks and Playgrounds Around the World 28
Glossary 30
Bibliography 31
Read More 31
Learn More Online 31
Index 32
About the Author 32

Eerie Parks and Playgrounds

Darkness **descends** on an empty playground. A swing slowly begins to sway back and forth. Is the wind pushing it? Soon, the swing flies higher and higher in the air. Yet no one is around. Suddenly, there's the pitter-patter of small feet and the faint sound of a child's laughter. Has a spirit come out to play?

Parks and playgrounds are inviting places where you can play and enjoy the outdoors. However, these **picturesque** places often hide terrible secrets. Some are the sites of all-too-real **tragedies**. Others are home to ghostly terrors. If you visit one of the parks or playgrounds in this book, you may catch **glimpses** of the living dead.

A Spooky Swing

Playground, Firmat, Argentina

At first glance, Firmat, Argentina, looks like any other small city. However, there's a children's playground that has the whole city spooked.

The spooky playground in Firmat, Argentina

In June 2007, **residents** noticed something strange at a local playground. A swing was rapidly moving back and forth. Yet nobody was on it. The people wondered: *Is it being pushed by the wind?* Then, for ten days in a row, the swing kept moving on its own—even on windless days. *Creak, creak. Creak, creak. Creak, creak.*

Concerned locals asked the police to **investigate**. After examining the swing, the officers had no idea what was causing it to move on its own. They found no strings tied to the swing—or anything else unusual about it. Even when the police stopped the swing from moving, it quickly picked up **momentum** again.

All the while, teachers, parents, and children had their own explanation. "We believe it's haunted," says Maria de Silva Agustina, a local teacher. According to one **legend**, a child was accidentally killed on a construction site not far from where the swing set was built. Could this explain why the spooky swing would never stop . . . or was it really just the wind? The question remains.

The police contacted a team of scientists to uncover the mystery. They were **stumped** as well.

Haunted Hawaii

MacKenzie State Park, The Big Island, Hawaii

This small park is tucked away under a grove of tall trees on a **volcanic** island. Hardened black **lava** covers the ground like a death **shroud**. What unearthly creatures roam around the area?

MacKenzie State Park

In the 1800s, prisoners were forced to work in the park, which is located on the Big Island. Swinging pickaxes, they carved out trails in the hard ground. Long after they died, their ghosts are said to still wander the park. The shadowy figures appear half starved and unshaven, dragging tools behind them.

According to reports, campers in the park have been awakened by bloodcurdling screams. Sometimes, an unseen force unzips their sleeping bags. "That place, I really believe is haunted," says one visitor. "I just got goosebumps thinking about it."

In addition to the ghosts of dead prisoners, **native** Hawaiians believe the park is home to "night marchers." These spirits of long-dead Hawaiians supposedly march along the trails during the night. They grasp ghostly torches and pound drums. If you see them, locals say you should drop to the ground and hold still. That's the only way the spirits will spare your life.

On the blackest nights, the spirit of a former prisoner called Louie is said to appear to visitors. It's believed that he killed another **inmate** and later died in the park.

A Deadly Storm

De Soto Grade School Playground, De Soto, Illinois

Chilling cries ring out in a school playground in De Soto. Long ago, a terrible storm changed the village forever—and it might have also unleashed a wave of restless spirits.

De Soto Grade School before the storm

On Wednesday, March 18, 1925, one of the deadliest tornadoes in U.S. history ripped through the state of Illinois. The powerful storm tore train tracks from the ground and flattened buildings. It uprooted huge trees and shot them into the air like giant arrows.

At De Soto Grade School, the teachers and students watched the skies turn black. Moments later, the tornado's strong winds shattered the building's windows. Screaming children ran for their lives. Then the unthinkable happened. The top floor of the school collapsed. The children were struck by hurtling bricks. Many were crushed to death. A small girl was picked up by the winds and thrown over 1,000 feet (305 m). In all, 33 children lost their lives.

Since the deadly tornado, the village of De Soto built a new school and playground on the site of the old building. Residents have seen **apparitions** of children wearing dusty, torn clothes playing on the playground. Their screams and cries can be heard for miles, especially on stormy nights.

The 1925 tornado in De Soto killed more children than any other tornado in U.S. history.

De Soto Grade School after the tornado

Watch Your Step!

Hummel Park, Omaha, Nebraska

Hummel Park stretches for hundreds of spooky, wooded acres. Stone steps lead to quiet walking trails. The park may look picture-perfect. However, it holds horrible secrets.

Hummel Park is said to be one of the spookiest spots in Nebraska. Some people say that the park's famously mysterious stone staircase is cursed. Called the **Morphing** Stairs, visitors claim that the number of steps changes, depending on whether a person is walking up the stairs or down them.

Other visitors have sworn they've seen strange-looking people with bright white hair wandering around the park at night. Still others mention a **hermit** who lives in a tiny house in the woods. It's said that he'll make a meal out of anything that breathes.

In addition to these dark legends, terrible things have actually happened in the park. Between 1933 and 2006, three people were found dead there.

Is the park haunted? "Go out there at midnight and see how uneasy you feel," says a man who lives near the park. "You'll hear noises you don't normally think possible."

In 1930, a wealthy family donated 202 acres (82 hectares) of land to the city of Omaha. The area later became Hummel Park.

The Morphing Stairs

Grave Matters

Weccacoe Playground, Philadelphia, Pennsylvania

On a warm summer day, children play hide-and-seek at a popular Philadelphia playground. They scramble to find the best hiding places. Little do they know that beneath their feet is a graveyard!

Weccacoe Playground

In the 1800s, there were laws in Philadelphia that kept African-Americans from being buried in the city. Richard Allen, a freed slave, wanted to change that. After he founded a church in the south part of Philadelphia, he bought land for a cemetery for his church members. He called the graveyard Mother Bethel Burial Ground. Over a period of 60 years, more than 5,000 African-Americans were laid to rest there.

By the 1860s, the church had stopped burying people in the cemetery. It became overgrown with weeds and was totally forgotten about. In 1889, the city bought the land and turned it into the Weccacoe Playground. In 2013, while the playground was being **renovated**, the burial ground was rediscovered. Workers uncovered human bones and pieces of broken gravestones. Locals were stunned. One gravestone read: "Whosoever lives and believeth in me, though we be dead, yet shall we live."

In 2018, the city built a **memorial** in the playground to honor the people buried there.

The word *weccacoe* comes from the language of Lenape Native Americans. It means "peaceful place."

Creepy in Connecticut

Boothe Memorial Park and Museum, Stratford, Connecticut

For decades, Boothe Park has been the talk of the town. This pretty spot with its quirky buildings is an inviting place for a picnic—and a heart-pounding scare.

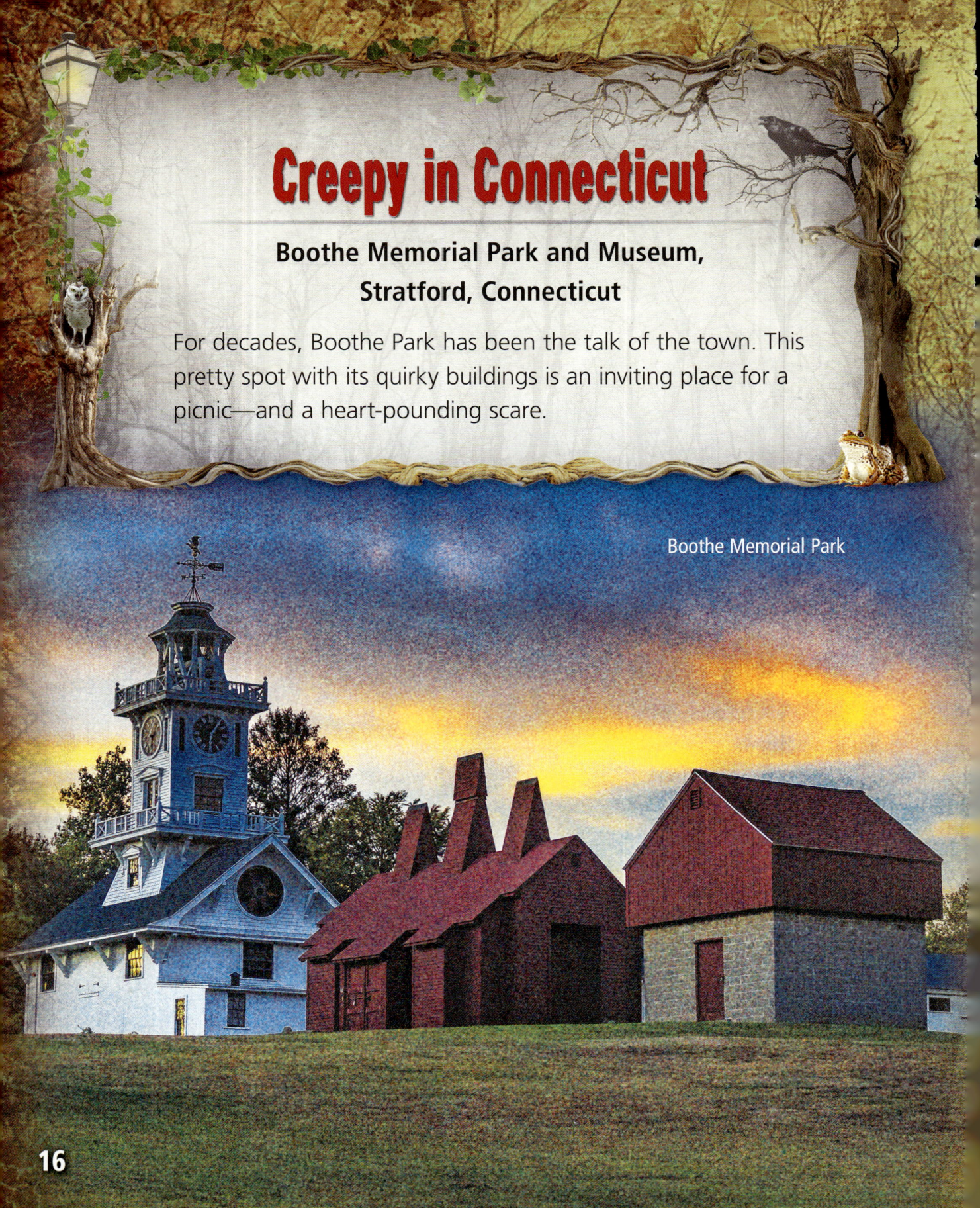

Boothe Memorial Park

The Boothe family built a large home in Stratford in the mid-1800s. In the early 1900s, Boothe family members turned the estate into a park—and a **shrine** to the bizarre.

The property contains a collection of unusual buildings. There's a mini-windmill, clock tower, lighthouse, trolley station, chapel, and an odd building that has no windows or doors. There's also an old cemetery connected to the park. Aside from being an all-around strange place, the cemetery has been the site of many ghostly encounters. The most common is the vision of a hooded figure standing on top of the clock tower. Long-dead Boothe family members have also been spotted on the grounds near the cemetery.

One of the most frightening events took place in the cemetery in the 1990s. A visitor walking among the headstones felt sharp stabbing pains in his back and fell to the ground. He later found out that the grave he had fallen on belonged to a Boothe family member who had been stabbed to death!

A visitor to Boothe Memorial Park took a photo of one of the empty buildings. When she looked at the photo at a later time, she saw a ghostly face peering back at her from the picture!

Sick to Death

Pine Hills, Orlando, Florida

Tucked on a quiet street in the Pine Hills neighborhood of Orlando is a large park and playground. Why is it always empty? Perhaps it's because it was built on the site of a hospital of horrors.

Sunland Hospital

Sunland Hospital was built in the 1950s to treat people with a deadly lung disease called tuberculosis. Then, in 1967, it became a hospital for mentally ill people. Conditions at the hospital were horrific. It was overcrowded and **infested** with bugs and rats. One patient remembers waking up to find a huge rat sitting on her chest! Eventually, the hospital was shut down. For 15 years, it stood empty . . . except for a few ghosts.

One of the ghosts was a deeply upset young boy. He had been seen running from empty room to empty room. Then he paused to look around. Who or what was he looking for? No one will ever know. Another apparition was a scared young girl. Her mouth was wide open as if she were trying to scream—yet no sound came out. One day, a witness saw her walk toward a window and hurl herself out of it.

In 1999, the hospital was finally torn down, and a park and playground were built in its place. The ghosts remain, however. Visitors have reported seeing **spectral** figures in hospital gowns and hearing screams in the dead of night.

In 1997, a curious young man visited the **abandoned** hospital with friends. He accidentally fell down an empty elevator shaft and nearly died.

Garden of Good and Evil

Untermyer Park, Yonkers, New York

Situated on a hillside along the Hudson River, this park has lovely gardens . . . and killer views. It's said to have once been the hangout of an **infamous** murderer.

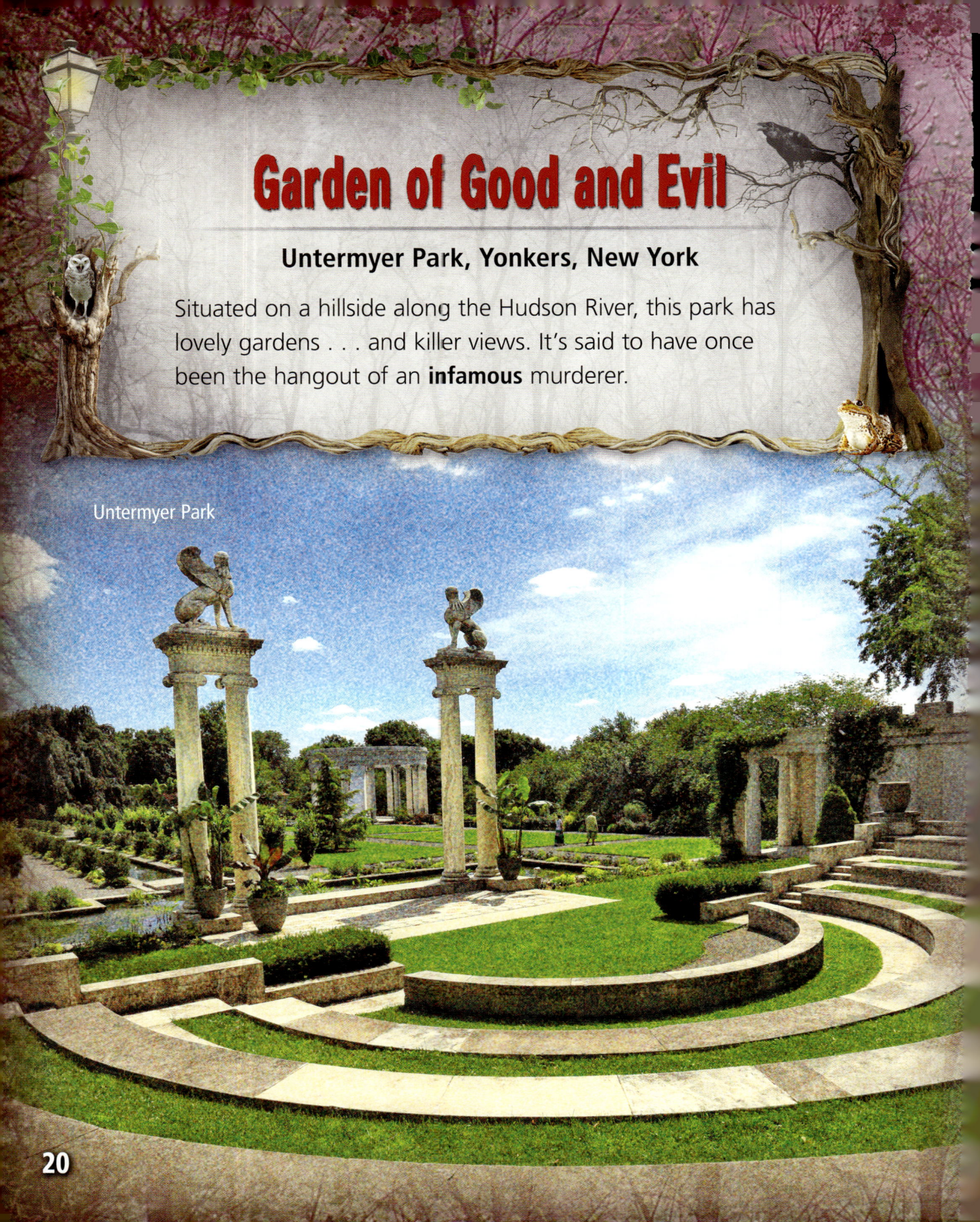

Untermyer Park

Born in 1858, Samuel Untermyer was a wealthy and respected lawyer. He lived in a grand estate, where he built one of the finest gardens in the country. It included thousands of flowers and huge fountains. Samuel even designed a living **sundial** made from different plants.

After Samuel died in 1940, the gardens fell into **disrepair**. For three decades, the once beautiful grounds became a tangle of weeds. That's when locals began hearing strange chanting coming from the area. Then police started finding dead, skinned animals in and around the park. They believed that a **cult** was visiting the property at night. It's said that one of the cult members was David Berkowitz, also known as the Son of Sam. He was sent to prison in 1978 for murdering six people!

Today, the park is once again a beautiful place. However, some people believe that the cult members return when the moon is full.

Every Tuesday, Samuel Untermyer opened his garden to the public. Once, in 1939, more than 30,000 people came to visit!

David Berkowitz

Troubled Waters

Golden Gate Park, San Francisco, California

Golden Gate Park, which covers over 1,000 acres (405 hectares), offers an escape from the city of San Francisco. When the fog rolls in, however, the park transforms. It turns into a place where a **grieving** ghost roams.

Stow Lake at Golden Gate Park

It was a beautiful day in the early 1900s. According to legend, a young mother went for a walk in Golden Gate Park. She pushed her baby in a stroller around Stow Lake, which sparkled in the sunshine. Suddenly, the woman spotted an old friend. They sat down on a bench to talk. The mother parked the stroller beside her. She excitedly chatted with her friend, and then turned to check on her baby. The stroller was gone! She jumped up and ran around the lake, screaming for her lost child. Then she **plunged** into the lake to look for her baby—and was never seen alive again.

Is the story true? No one knows for sure. However, for over 100 years, people have reported seeing a glowing figure on foggy nights. She's dressed in white and nervously circles the lake. Sometimes, she's seen rising from the center of the lake. She often asks people to help her find her baby. Some believe if you say yes, she'll haunt you forever.

In 1906, two young girls reported seeing a baby floating in Golden Gate Park. Was it the mother's long-lost baby? We'll never know. Police did not find the baby's body.

Dead Children's Playground

Drost Park, Huntsville, Alabama

If you take a walk in Alabama's Maple Hill Cemetery, you might stumble upon something very unusual. There's a playground right next to the graves! It's no surprise that locals call it Dead Children's Playground.

Drost Park, also known as Dead Children's Playground

Maple Hill Cemetery is the largest and oldest cemetery in Alabama. It was founded in 1822 and covers over 100 acres (40 hectares) of land. In 1918, during a flu outbreak, many children died and were buried there. Today, it contains 80,000 bodies. Curiously, the city of Huntsville decided to build a park and playground right next to the cemetery.

Tall, rocky cliffs surround the playground on three sides. It's also tucked under a group of large trees, so it's almost always dark and gloomy. At night, however, the place goes from gloomy to ghostly. For years, people have spotted blurry figures playing on the swing set and jungle gym. Eyes are seen glowing in the cliffs. Dust sometimes rises from the footsteps of unseen children. Most curious of all may be the **orbs** of light that float at what appears to be the same height as boys and girls. Do the spirits belong to children who were buried in the cemetery?

Legend says that during the 1960s, many children were kidnapped in and around Huntsville. The bodies of some of the children were discovered near where the playground now sits.

The Skunk Ape

Everglades National Park, Florida

The Everglades is a big swamp in southern Florida. Giant snakes slither along the ground. Huge alligators lurk in the murky water. However, some people have seen a creature that's more terrifying than all the rest!

Everglades National Park

Dave Shealy was ten years old when he first saw a skunk ape in 1974. "It was walking across the swamp," he now says. "It looked like a man, but was completely covered with hair." Dave was unable to believe his own eyes. According to Dave, the Bigfoot-like creatures can be up to 7 feet (2 m) tall and weigh as much as 450 pounds (204 kg). They are covered in shaggy red or black hair and walk on two legs. Skunk apes earned their name because of their horrible smell. People have compared the stink to that of rotting garbage or the smell of dead animals baking in the sun.

Dave says that skunk apes mostly eat berries, baby birds, and other small animals. However, they have been known to kill large wild boars—and who knows what else. Dave invites people to come and see for themselves what mysterious creatures are lurking in the Everglades. If you smell something rotten, look no further than your nose. It might be a skunk ape!

A skunk ape is known as a cryptid, an animal whose existence has not yet been proven.

Dave Shealy has studied skunk apes for his entire life. He says that the creatures love lima beans and the taste of deer liver!

Eerie Parks and Playgrounds

Hummel Park
Omaha, Nebraska

This wooded park may be one of Nebraska's most haunted places.

De Soto Grade School Playground
De Soto, Illinois

Beware of the spirits of tornado victims at this playground.

Weccacoe Playground
Philadelphia, Pennsylvania

This playground was built on top of a cemetery!

Golden Gate Park
San Francisco, California

Is a grieving ghost haunting this foggy park?

MacKenzie State Park
The Big Island, Hawaii

Are there more ghosts or visitors at this creepy park?

Everglades National Park
Florida

Find out what stinky creature is lurking in this swamp.

Pine Hills
Orlando, Florida

From horror hospital to playground—it's no wonder this place is empty.

Playground
Firmat, Argentina

A creepy swing has a life of its own.

28

Around the World

Boothe Memorial Park and Museum
Stratford, Connecticut
This quirky park hides many dark secrets.

Untermyer Park
Yonkers, New York
Beautiful garden or satanic meeting place? This park has a tale to tell.

Drost Park
Huntsville, Alabama
The name "Dead Children's Playground" says it all.

Arctic Ocean

EUROPE

ASIA

AFRICA

Indian Ocean

AUSTRALIA

Southern Ocean

ANTARCTICA

Glossary

abandoned (uh-BAN-duhnd) no longer in use

apparitions (ah-puh-RISH-uhnz) ghosts or ghostlike images

cult (KUHLT) a group of people who have religious beliefs or practices thought to be strange or harmful

descends (di-SENDZ) moves or falls downward

disrepair (dis-rih-PAIR) poor condition due to neglect

glimpses (GLIMP-sez) brief or partial views

grieving (GREEV-ing) feeling very sad after a loss

hermit (HUR-mit) a person who lives alone and away from the rest of the world

infamous (IN-fuh-muss) well-known for something very bad

infested (in-FESS-tihd) overrun with lots of insects or animals that can cause harm

inmate (IN-mayt) someone who has been sent to prison

investigate (in-VESS-tuh-gayt) to search for information about something

lava (LAH-vuh) hot, liquid rock that comes out of a volcano

legend (LEJ-uhnd) a story from the past that's often not entirely true

memorial (muh-MOR-ee-uhl) something built to honor or remember people or events

momentum (moh-MEN-tuhm) the force or speed of movement

morphing (MAWR-fing) changing slowly from one thing to another

native (NAY-tiv) born in a particular place

orbs (AWRBS) glowing spheres

picturesque (pik-chur-REHSK) charming or pretty to look at

plunged (PLUNJD) entered suddenly

renovated (REH-nuh-vay-tid) improved the condition of something

residents (REZ-uh-dehnts) people who live in a particular place

shrine (SHRYNE) a building associated with holiness

shroud (SHROWD) a cloth in which a dead person is wrapped for burial

spectral (SPEK-truhl) like a ghost

stumped (STUHMPD) unable to work out what to do or say

sundial (SUHN-dye-ill) an instrument that tells the time of day by using shadows

tragedies (TRAH-juh-deez) terrible or sad events

volcanic (vol-KAN-ik) formed by a volcano, a kind of mountain that shoots out melted rock and ash

Bibliography

Austin, Joanne. *Weird Hauntings: True Tales of Ghostly Places.* New York: Sterling (2006).

Hauck, Dennis William. *Haunted Places: The National Directory: Ghostly Abodes, Sacred Sites, UFO Landings, and Other Supernatural Locations.* New York: Penguin (2002).

Read More

Markovics, Joyce. *Haunted Gotham (Scary Places:Cities).* New York: Bearport (2017).

Stern, Steven L. *Cursed Grounds (Scary Places).* New York: Bearport (2011).

Williams, Dinah. *Spooky Cemeteries (Scary Places).* New York: Bearport (2008).

Learn More Online

To learn more about eerie parks and playgrounds, visit
www.bearportpublishing.com/ScaryPlaces

Index

Boothe Memorial Park and Museum 16–17, 29

cemeteries 15, 17, 24–25, 28

Dead Children's Playground 24–25, 29
De Soto Grade School Playground 10–11, 28
De Soto, Illinois 10–11, 28
Drost Park 24–25, 29

Everglades National Park 26–27, 28

Firmat, Argentina 6–7, 28
Florida 18, 26–27, 28

gardens 20–21, 29
Golden Gate Park 22–23, 28

Hawaii 8–9, 28
Hummel Park 12–13, 28
Huntsville, Alabama 24–25, 29

MacKenzie State Park 8–9, 28
Maple Hill Cemetery 24–25

Omaha, Nebraska 12–13, 28
orbs 25, 30
Orlando, Florida 18–19, 28

Philadelphia, Pennsylvania 14–15, 28
Pine Hills 18–19, 28
prisoners 9

San Francisco, California 22, 28
skunk ape 26–27
Stratford, Connecticut 16–17, 29
Sunland Hospital 18–19

tornado 10–11, 28

Untermyer Park 20–21, 29
Untermyer, Samuel 21

Weccacoe Playground 14–15, 28

About the Author

Joyce Markovics is a children's book author who lives in a very old house that may or may not be haunted. She would like to dedicate this book to Jake Goldberg, a very special guy who loves all things spooky.